To Sandy,

Thought you might enjoy the
very warm and lovely watercolors
of the Southwest, especially.

Christmas 1990

Chris + Steve

A WRITER'S EYE

Harry N. Abrams, Inc., Publishers, New York

A WRITER'S EYE

FIELD NOTES AND WATERCOLORS
BY PAUL HORGAN

With an Introduction by David McCullough

Editor: RUTH A. PELTASON
Designer: ANA ROGERS

*Photographs by Joseph Szaszfai with the exception of the following: Robert Nugent, pages
33, 34 and 85, M. Skelton, pages 38 and 82.
Unless otherwise noted, the illustrations are from the Yale Collection of American Literature,
Beinecke Rare Book and Manuscript Library.*

*Editor's Note: As the chapter titles indicate, each chapter is based on a book by the author;
the quotations (with page references to the original editions) are taken from the
corresponding book.*

Library of Congress Cataloging-in-Publication Data

Horgan, Paul, 1903–
A writer's eye: field notes and watercolors / by Paul Horgan;
with an introduction by David McCullough.
p.   cm.
ISBN 0–8109–1792–0
1. Horgan, Paul, 1903–
2. Watercolor painting, American.
3. Watercolor painting—20th century—United States.
4. United States in art.
I. Title.
ND1839.H64A4   1987   87–17369
CIP
7.59.13—dc19

Text copyright © 1988 Paul Horgan
Introduction copyright © 1988 David McCullough
Illustrations copyright © 1988 Paul Horgan

Published in 1988 by Harry N. Abrams, Incorporated, New York
All rights reserved. No part of the contents of this book may be
reproduced without the written permission of the publisher

A Times Mirror Company

Printed and bound in Japan

Title page: *Gas for lighting, Santa Fe, 1880 (after old photograph)*

CONTENTS

To
Henriette
And
In Memory Of
Peter

PREFACE

Writing from Paris on 30 April 1821 to his friend Charles Soulier in Italy, Eugène Delacroix said, "You'll go to Naples, no doubt, that loveliest and saddest region on earth. I advise you, as strongly as possible, not to neglect the slightest sketch you can find time to make. Your whole journey will live again in these notes. A drawing, however faint and indistinct, is better than the most accurate description. . . . You will be storing up a keen delight for yourself."

With the natural grace of his enthusiasm and the power of his vocation, Delacroix, whose gift with the writing pen was as evocative as his genius with the brush, was making out of his natural bias a case for the graphic as against the verbal uses of description. Yet in his own unity of expression he stands as an example of the artist who commands word and image with equal felicity. His animated correspondence and the leaping span of his wonderful journal breathe forth the strong beauty of his nature and the bold, clear, and charming play of his vision. The same qualities shine out from his watercolor sketches—for example, his scenes taken in Morocco. He is the brilliant conveyor of the immediate, and he has long been my consolation in my amateur attempts to bring unity out of the separate means of drawing and writing, to the aid of literary and historical work.

While I have always enjoyed making drawings—mostly in India ink and watercolor—and while something of that enjoyment may now and then reach out to a viewer as it has to various collectors of my small pictures, the point of the present selection, accompanied by supporting text, is to illustrate one of the means by which I have pursued my field studies in preparation for the writing of certain of my books. These are *Great River: The Rio Grande in North American History*, *Conquistadors in North American History*, and *Lamy of Santa Fe: His Life and Times*.

In most cases the final texts of my three books reflect visual impressions of places or objects drawn during my research travels; but some of the drawings relate to broader responses to landscape, buildings, or objects that I wanted to retain as elements of entire atmospheres or cultures, and so to bring me a comprehensive feeling that might find its way into the flavor of my written pages. As written notes often have a general rather than a specific usefulness for the writer, so with my drawings.

This is not to ignore the resonant value of unrecorded observations—those facts and strikes of imagination which remain, and recur, as experience itself. They might be called the residue of echoing truth. Their lingering power preserves general atmospheres against which enlivening details stand in relief as suggestive fragments of the past. The writer of history or biography who tries to see places as they might have been in earlier days can give to old and elusive airs the feeling almost of present time.

It was long my habit, then, to supplement my general observations with drawings of places or objects as notes related to historical subjects. My purpose was to make a record of what I saw as clearly as I could set it down. Whether my drawings would show other people what I saw was not my main concern — though I was gratified when they seemed to recognize a place which we both knew. My main concern was to have a graphic note which later on would not only show me what I saw but would remind me of how I felt when I saw it. It was in the revival of this feeling that the value of my preparatory drawings existed for me.

Urgency always attended the making of them. When I saw a subject that gave reality to something I would write about, I could not get at it with cool control. I must grasp it before my emotion of discovery and recognition could fade. Often I found my subject by coming on it while driving my car; and often, as I parked facing it, I left the engine running as though to spur my urgency to get on with the drawing in all possessed haste before the first impact of my subject should have worn off. I went at the paper with my India ink fountain pen, establishing the observed facts in outline; and then with watercolors I tried to capture light, form, atmosphere, harmony, and the scheme of values in the near and far.

Excitement attended the process, and something of that excitement returned when I looked at the drawings later; and when I treated the same subjects in words, perhaps the words were more true and evocative as a result.

P.H.

Middletown,
Connecticut.

INTRODUCTION

by

David McCullough

PUBLICATION OF PAUL HORGAN'S
wonderfully expressive watercolors, his "field notes" as he modestly calls them, is a high occasion, not only for what they reveal about his approach to his writing, or for the pleasure they give quite on their own, but for all they add to our appreciation of an amazing, creative life. He is so many things, this remarkable man—novelist, historian, biographer, teacher, bookman, critic, brilliant talker, and, as these pages show, a gifted painter. Looking through a biographical file, I am reminded of how manifold is even his full name, Paul George Vincent O'Shaughnessy Horgan.

Critical recognition came early, more than fifty years ago. Since, he has been compared to Tolstoy, Henry James, and Thomas Hardy. He is the writer's writer, the biographer's biographer. "No writer has more honorable credentials," Walker Percy has said. Leon Edel calls Horgan's *Lamy of Santa Fe* one of the great American biographies of all time. Henry Steele Commager includes Horgan the historian in the "goodly company" of Gibbon, Macaulay, and Francis Parkman.

The career began with a book of drawings, interestingly. It was a juvenile called *Men of Arms* depicting warriors through history. It was published in 1931. The first novel, *The Fault of Angels*, appeared two years later. In all he has written seventeen novels. He has published four volumes of short stories, five works of biography, several histories, another juvenile, a book on writing, an anthology of his work called *Of America East and West* that appeared in 1984—more than forty books in total and these, as he explains, built on an apprenticeship of five early novels that he discarded. He never lets up. Invariably, he has three or four "projects" going, as he does at this writing, and invariably he refuses to talk about them until finished.

The most widely acclaimed of his histories is *Great River*, an epic, two-volume chronicle of civilization in the valley of the Rio Grande, a true magnum opus that is both a monumental work of scholarship and a literary masterpiece. Published in 1954, it received the Bancroft and Pulitzer prizes. Twenty years later, for his *Lamy of Santa Fe*, the life of Archbishop Jean Baptiste Lamy, he received a second Pulitzer Prize.

He has, besides, lectured at Yale, the University of Iowa, and Wesleyan University at Middletown, Connecticut, where for a number of years he headed the Center for Advanced Studies and where he still makes his home. He has been a Book-of-the-Month Club judge, chairman of the Santa Fe Opera, a fellow of the Morgan Library. If I have counted correctly, he has twenty honorary degrees, and this apart from the fact that he never went to college.

If a man can be known by the company he keeps, consider his friends down the years, east and west. They have included Frank Capra and Allan Nevins, Henry Steele Commager, C. P. Snow, Father Theodore Hesburgh, the ballerina Vera Zorina, Senator Daniel Patrick Moynihan, Edmund Wilson, and Igor Stravinsky, who was the subject of one of Paul's most engaging books. Robert Oppenheimer was a boyhood pal in New Mexico. And so was the painter Peter Hurd, who later brought Paul into the fold of the numerous Wyeth family of Chadds Ford, Pennsylvania, when Hurd married the oldest Wyeth daughter, Henriette, who still talks with Paul almost weekly by phone from the Hurd ranch in San Patricio, New Mexico.

"His devotion is so warm and dazzling and profound," she has said. "He is always giving. Most people don't, you know. People can be so pinched and cold. Paul is always giving."

Paul is past eighty, but as he once wrote of Stravinsky, his age is the least relevant detail about him.

He was born in Buffalo, New York, August 1, 1903, the second of three children in a close-knit, affluent family of strong Catholic faith and tremendous creative vitality. "Everybody around me was talented and gave everybody talent. Everybody painted. My mother had a beautiful voice. My father was a marvelous drawing-room actor." Yet even in such company, Paul stood out. Indeed, he was judged so versatile by family and friends that they thought he might never amount to anything.

The Horgan side was Irish. His adored father, Edward Daniel Horgan, was vice president of a printing business owned by Paul's maternal grandfather, a stately old German with the memorable name of Matthias Rohr. (He is Grosspa in the superb novel *Things as They Are*, where Paul's father and mother also figure.)

In 1915, when Paul was twelve, his father, who had contracted tuberculosis, gave up his business and moved the family to the high, dry spaces of New Mexico. In 1923, two years after his father's death, twenty-year-old Paul Horgan came east again, to Rochester, New York, and the Eastman School of Music—resolved to be an artist, but whether a singer, painter, actor, or writer, he wasn't sure. He had reason to be puzzled since he could sing, paint, act, and write.

For the moment he settled on singing instructions, but ultimately chose to be a writer, because, as he explains, only as a writer could he make use of all four talents. A writer must see with the painter's eye, a

A sixteenth-century Spanish courtier (after a painting by Sanchez Coello)

FACES from the GOLDEN AGE of SPAIN

Franciscans
after Herrera the Elder
(1576-1656)

a layman.
after Herrera

Spanish faces, sixteenth century (after paintings by Herrera the Elder)

writer must have an ear for the music of words, the actor's gift for mimicry, the capacity to take any part.

"I am everyone in my novels," he says. "If this were not so, no one in my novels would have a chance to ring true. . . ." Recalling the youthful Paul Horgan who visited on vacations at the Wyeth home in Chadds Ford, Henriette Wyeth Hurd says, "He could become Louis XIV in an instant. Or put on a hat and be Napoleon or Washington, depending on how he pinched the hat."

The singing instructions ended after a year, but he stayed on in Rochester for another two years as a set designer and production assistant for the Eastman Theater under Rouben Mamoulian, who, with artist N. C. Wyeth, patriarch of the Wyeth family, had the greatest early influence on him.

It was Wyeth who arranged for the publication of his first book of drawings, *Men of Arms*. "He took me seriously. He treated me as an equal—though there were light years between his level and mine. He allowed me the dignity of effort . . . gave me the sense my powers would grow."

In 1926, resettled in New Mexico, he began to write seriously, supporting himself as librarian at the New Mexico Military Institute in Roswell, the school he had attended. Except for the years of the Second World War, when he served as chief of the Army Information Branch in Washington, New Mexico remained his home for nearly forty years, until the early 1960s, when he moved to Connecticut.

The east-west halves of his life, the continuing play of east and west through his writing, may seem divisive. At least one close student of his work has seen exile in the west as a central theme. But Horgan's east and west are a creative arc. Repeatedly, in the novels, the histories and biographies, his principal characters are people who go far, literally and figuratively. To appreciate how far, it is essential we know from where they began, and so origins are always important in Horgan's view of life. Archbishop Lamy's beginnings in France, for example, are as vital to an understanding of the full man as are the empty landscapes and crystal skies of frontier New Mexico where Lamy did his great work. And here, of course, the creative arc is not merely continental in scale.

An authentic sense of place is paramount for this writer. It is why the act of drawing has such value for him. He isn't just "doing research," he is entering heart and mind into the spirit of setting. Drawing demands that, and his swift, concentrated kind most of all. The lovely, deceptively simple watercolor view of Clermont-Ferrand and its double-spired cathedral on page 71, is at once the spontaneous impression of an American traveler and what later, for the purposes of biography, "informed" these lines:

> From childhood, Jean Baptiste Lamy, gazing from the tilled fields well to the north of Lempdes, across bluing hills, to the farthest line of the land where the solitary profile of the Puy-de-Dôme rose in the distance, could see between near and far the hazy cluster of the city of Clermont-Ferrand. The only constant and distinguishable features which he could pick out were the two spires of the cathedral side by side, there, at the end of the country road leading from Lempdes to the city and the world. At that angle, in certain airs and lights, they might fancifully suggest the twin spires of a mitre, such as worn by a bishop, a lord and teacher.

Landscape is important, he knows, because landscape is so often character. It is so often joined with destiny. In an introduction to three of the southwest novels, *Main Line West, Far from Cibola,* and *The Common Heart,* published under the title, *Mountain Standard Time,* he has this to say: "It is the land of the prairie farmer. If his world is flat, so too may be his spirit, his voice, his private containment within a human horizon of drought-like shrewdness, all of which must affect his family and they in turn their society."

Courage is a prevailing theme in nearly all he has written — but it is courage derived from faith or from experience, like the boy in *Things as They Are* who is afraid of the lightning. Courage combined with intelligence is best of all.

He never forgets the human stakes in a situation. He is fascinated by communities of all kinds, by "man's ways of constantly reshaping himself as a social being." Still, he prizes independence. There is the bugler in the robust novel *A Distant Trumpet*, young Olin Rainey, breaking away from his narrow house and alcoholic father to a life of uncertain freedom and adventure in the U.S. Cavalry. Or Igor Stravinsky, who must remain independent of casual friendships.

Light is a prevailing fascination. He works with light — with his "writer's eye." Again and again we encounter "bright drops of light" . . . "beads of light" . . . "golden afternoon sunlight" . . . "the delicate restrained light of Sunday afternoon" . . . "furious sunlight" . . . lamplight in windows, lamplight spilling in pools over tables and chairs.

And he is brilliant at portraiture, as a writer who paints would be. This is how he introduces King Charles I of Spain in *Great River:*

King Charles, who was also the Holy Roman Emperor, lived and worked in hard bare rooms with no carpets, crowding to the fire in winter, using the window's sunshine in summer. The doctors of medicine stated that the humors of moisture and of cold dominated his quality. His face was fixed in calm, but for his eyes, which moved and spoke more than his gestures or his lips. His face was pale and long, the lower lip full and forward, often dry and cracked so that he kept on it a green leaf to suck. His nose was flat and his brows were pitted with a raised frown that

Roma, Texas, on the lower Rio Grande—store of M. Guerra

appeared to suggest a constant headache. He held his shoulders high as though on guard. He would seem to speak twice, once within and fully, and then outwardly and meagerly. But his eyes showed his mind, brilliant, deep, and always at work. He loved information for its own sake, was always reading, and knew his maps well. They said he saw the Indies better than many who went there, and held positive views on all matters concerning the New World and its conquerors.

Horgan's prodigious work has ranged across four hundred years of history. He has written of opera, theater, music, painting, politics, war, American and European letters, Abraham Lincoln and Willa Cather, the natural sciences, church history, intellectual history—and much that is cruel or tragic in everyday life. I think of the retarded child in the chapter titled "Muzza" in *Things as They Are*, or the dreadful hardships, violence, and bigotry, the prevailing loneliness portrayed in *Far from Cibola*, his vivid novel of the Great Depression. All the failings of humankind are well within his large vision.

In spirit, in tone he can be brisk, funny, Biblical, arch, or down-to-earth. And elegant, as in this line from the novel *No Quarter Given* describing two characters from the New York theater: "They arose, and folded their pride or their furies around themselves, and went, each the axis upon which a world spun." He can render a character, or an entire age, with a single deftly chosen quote, as when he tells of the brutal Spanish conqueror dying of his wounds who, when asked where he hurt the most, replied, "In my soul." Or Winfield Scott's comment on Zachary Taylor that "few men ever had a more comfortable, labor-saving contempt for learning of any kind."

Strongest perhaps is his gift of empathy. It is what, more than anything, makes it possible for him to carry us into other times and other peoples' lives, real or imagined.

He talks of the gratification in submerging one's self in a large purpose. His work is a calling, even an act of devotion, one senses. Certainly the moral choices at the center of life are central to what he writes. He is all in all a profoundly moral writer and though his religious views are never paraded, he is not unlike the seventeenth-century Spaniards he describes in *Great River*, for whom faith is a condition of their very being.

They believed that, with the love of God, nothing failed; without it, nothing prospered. . . . Thus seeking their love across mountain and strand, neither gathering flowers nor fearing beasts, they would pass fortress and frontier, able to endure all because of their strength of spirit in companionship of their Divine Lord.

Such belief existed within the Spanish not as a compartment where they kept their worship and faith, but as a condition of their very being, like the touch by which they felt the solid world, and the breath of life they drew until they died. It was the simplest and yet the most significant fact about them, and more than any other accounted for their achievement in the New World. With mankind's imperfect material—for they knew all their failings, indeed, revelled in them and beat themselves with them and knew death was too good for them if Christ had to suffer so much thorn and lance and nail for them—they yet could strive to fulfill the divine will, made plain to them by the Church. Relief from man's faulty nature could be had only in God. In obedience to Him, they found their greatest freedom, the essential freedom of the personality, the individual spirit in the self, with all its other expressions which they knew well—irony, extravagance, romance, vividness and poetry in speech, and honor, and hard pride.

"The mystery which lies at the heart of literature," he has said, "must be related to love—love of subject, love of the act of work, love of the human mind and its desire to be informed. . . ."

In the craft of history he has made his own way, self-taught like Parkman and Prescott, and like them he has raised the writing of history to the level of literature. His *Great River* and *Lamy of Santa Fe*, the works, as it happens, which were most "informed" by his drawings, will, I am sure, be read a hundred years from now.

Of the art of fiction, inventive writing as he likes to call it, he has said, "He who fears to be out of mode does not deserve to belong to himself. Every imaginative production must contain some element of risk." (Once he mentioned to me his disappointment in rereading a certain American classic because he said the author showed no nerve.) "The most valuable writers," he says, "are those in whom we find not themselves, or ourselves, or the fugitive era of their lifetime, but the common vision of all times."

The place where so many of the books have been written and others are currently in progress is a large book-lined study, really two generous rooms made one, on the ground floor of an old brick carriage house at the edge of the Wesleyan campus. There are desks of differing sizes here and there, and two or three big tables, all surfaces submerged in notes and reference books, stacks of manuscript pages and several typewriters. It seems more like the facility for a staff—for all the several Paul Horgans. Mementos are scattered about, framed pictures of friends and of his sister, Rosemary, now deceased, who looks beautiful enough to have been a screen star, small paintings, and shopping bags spilling over with back correspondence and I don't know what all, a low table filled with literary medals, a coffee table stacked with new books sent to him by publishers. There are two big couches, a number of comfortable armchairs, a fireplace and mantelpiece lined with still more treasures, and the walls the whole way around are solid with books from floor to ceiling—possibly ten thousand books, he estimates.

I once asked what he would save first from the room if the house were on fire. He thought probably it would be the Moynihan topaz, as he calls it, a honey-colored topaz the size of a golf ball that he keeps on the same table with the literary medals. Senator and Mrs. Moynihan brought it to him from India some years ago.

Paul told me to put it to my eye and suddenly everything remarkable about the room was made infinitely more so, a magic multiple of images, vivid, full of surprise, and everything bathed in the gemstone's own warm, clear light. To call the effect kaleidoscopic is not enough. The room was transformed.

It is what he has done with his life's work. He is his own kind of Moynihan topaz, transforming the world around with his warmth, his clarity, his gifts of observation and brilliant command of language.

"Make me *see*!" said Dickens, as precept for the writer.

Paul has been called a regionalist, a Southwest writer. He has been called a Catholic writer and a traditionalist. No label suffices, as no label ever does for an important artist.

With his reach of mind, the inclusiveness of his interests, he celebrates the inclusiveness of creation. Reading him we are in the presence of both a great writer and a great affirming spirit.

"Affirmation was the theme of his life," he has written of Archbishop Lamy. Affirmation is the theme of Paul Horgan's life.

He is a civilized and civilizing force, independent, sure of his ground, industrious, *original*. And uncorrupted. In the words of the citation of his honorary degree from Yale, he has been unwavering in his disciplined allegiance to the highest traditions of civility and craftsmanship. For all who care about the course of American civilization he is, or should be, a star to steer by. He teaches by example that style isn't fancy footwork or tricks with mirrors. Style is substance. Manner and man are one and same.

Drawings for

GREAT RIVER:

THE RIO GRANDE

IN

NORTH AMERICAN

HISTORY

AT TWELVE YEARS OF AGE
I first saw the Rio Grande when my family took up residence in Albuquerque in 1915. The river bounded the town's western edge, and I soon became a creature of the brown waters that flowed from the Rocky Mountains far to the north. In my impressionable age, the physical splendors of the New Mexico landscape entered into me—piercing light from on high; sovereign thunderheads ten miles above; pink gold in fine sandy bottoms edged by cottonwood groves; great lazy heat of summer afternoons; grinding spring dust storms; veiled blue of distant mountains; mercifully undeveloped solitudes.

Whenever I returned to New Mexico in later years, I went to the river; and in time its other character—that of a grand course for the flow of history—seized my interest in another dimension. My book took form during ten years of study in recorded sources and from my own observations of the river lands, from the rise in Colorado to the estuary at the Gulf of Mexico. Three times I travelled the whole length—some eighteen hundred miles—of the river country, and I revisited certain places many more times to certify my vision of events there: it was a compelling duty to travel five hundred miles for a proper sentence.

To support my hundreds of written notes, I made nearly two hundred drawings of places, objects, atmospheres, from which to recover, when needed, impressions of actuality for my narrative.

Searching for the source tributaries of the Rio Grande in the Rocky Mountains of Colorado I came to the town of Creede, where silver strikes in 1889 created a mining boom. A clear little stream called Willow Creek was sluiced through the town and made its way downstream to join the river. What I saw of Creede looked like a "western" movie set. (v. *Great River*, p. 891)

In the lens-like atmosphere ▶ the nearby northern face of the Sandia Mountains seemed to exhale a blue morning radiance over the sandy foothills and the earthen run of the foreground river. Empty of creature life, the landscape spoke to me of the scene in earlier centuries through which I sought my long narrative.

Rio Grande Near San Felipe, New Mexico
1957.
Watercolor and India ink,
11 × 14".
Collection Mr. Charles D. Berke, Jr.,
Middletown, Connecticut

Creede, Colorado
1947.
India ink, colored pencil, Chinese white,
5⅞ × 5⅜"

Grande verau
San Felipe 1957. Pour Madame CDPB.

This courthouse in Old Town, Albuquerque, dated from the nineteenth century. When I was a reporter on the *Albuquerque Journal* in 1921 at the age of eighteen, I used to cover the news there. Later it became a school and finally was razed. When I drew this a few years before it came down, I fixed some period memories of the Rio Grande country.

Old Bernalillo County Courthouse, Albuquerque
15 March 1958.
Watercolor, India ink,
8½ × 10½".
Collection Mr. Charles D. Berke, Jr., Middletown, Connecticut

With the Rio Grande and Mexico behind me, I was facing El Paso and Mt. Franklin from the railroad yards that paralleled the river. As the bare rock mountain with its cloud shadows dominated the natural landscape, the Hilton Hotel rose above the cityscape. At El Paso the north-south course of the river turns southeastward to form the border that runs to the Gulf of Mexico—the border that both divides and connects Mexico and the United States.

Mount Franklin and El Paso
12 October 1947, noon.
Colored pencil, India ink,
7¾ × 11"

North of El Paso the river makes a sweeping double bend. In full daytime it might not be visible from the elevation of the highway to its east; but in a clear falling evening, with shadowed ground, and a lingering brightness above, I saw that the river was earth's channel for the light of the sky.

Double Bend of the Rio Grande Above El Paso, Texas
13 October 1947, 6:15 P.M.
India ink, colored pencil,
5¾ × 8¹/₁₆″

Dust in the air and gold in the sky at sunset over El Paso/Juárez on this evening. The mountains in Mexico and the Chevron station in El Paso polarized the scene—abiding antiquity in contrast to modern commerce.

El Paso Dusk
1971.
Watercolor, India ink, and Chinese white on notebook paper,
3½ × 5¾"

When General Pancho
Villa seized Juárez in 1916
"The citizens of El Paso
clustered on the tops of tall
buildings to view through
telescopes the bivouac fires
by night, and by day, the
drag of cannon and the
wander of little columns of
revolutionary troops.
Chihuahua . . . now be-
longed to Pancho Villa."
(page 912) Early in a dusty
day facing Juárez I saw how
the loose earth of the river's
course was drawn over all
things by the hot wind.

Dusty Day—Juárez
16 March 1951.
Watercolor,
8½ × 10½"

For many months in 1916 northern Mexico—Chihuahua State—was the stage for the bloody posturings of Pancho Villa. Looking across the river from El Paso, I could "see" the Mexicans in "the acrid pathos of their land," and think of "its habits of life, death, and war." Their song said,

Maybe they have guns and
  cannons,
Maybe they are a lot stronger.
We have only rocks and mountains—
But we know how to last longer.
(page 927)

Houses at Juárez
January 1949.
Watercolor, Chinese white, India ink,
7¾ × 10".
Collection Mrs. Vitya Vronsky-Babin

When I set out in 1947 on the first of my three full-length journeys along the river's course toward the Gulf of Mexico, this subject was the first I tried to capture. Here some crucial interplay of the place, the light, the distance, gave me a sense of mystery and challenge as I began my ten-year attempt to recover the river's chronicle across the centuries.

__From Fabens, Texas, Into North Mexico__
Second version (1983) of a drawing done in 1947.
India ink, watercolor, Chinese white,
8⅜ × 10⅞".
Collection Mr. Clark Kimball, Santa Fe, New Mexico

"Upstream the river had always been in touch with mountains, but they lay generally parallel to its course. In the Big Bend the river encountered mountains in a new and extraordinary way; for they lay, chain after chain of them, directly across its course as though to deny it passage to the sea. But the pull of the sea was stronger than rock. The Rio Grande with its shallow flow did not turn aside, or dam itself into a system of lakes, but for ages wore its way as an antecedent river through the escarpments as they rose. . . ." (page 897) The whole region became a realm of fantasy. I kept this suggestion after a rain shower near the Chisos Mountains.

Big Bend Landscape, Texas
18 May 1947, 5:30 P.M.
Colored pencil, India ink,
7¾ × 9¾"

Of the Big Bend prehistoric cave culture on the Rio Grande: "A body was buried in rock shelters or under piled rocks in the open. The limbs were gathered against the body and bound. A few of its meager possessions were placed with it—things to work with and to pray. Woven fibre matting was wrapped around all . . . and a blanket of cactus leaves, thick and bursting with sharp needles, was put to protect and cover. On a flat rock-face nearby was a [pictograph] that said 'hand,' and meant, 'forever.'" (page 73)

Child Burial, Big Bend Cave Culture
10 May 1947.
Drawn after an object in the Witte Museum, San Antonio.
India ink, colored pencil, Chinese white,
7¾ × 11"

rain
gray
blue
silver

brown
tan

ashy
lichen

darkening sun
above

level

rusty foreground
green bushes.

mouth of Santa Elena Cañon —
Big Bend · 19 may 1947. noon

Mouth of Santa Elena Canyon, Big Bend, Texas
19 May 1947, noon.
India ink, colored pencil, Chinese white,
7⅞ × 11⅛″

Of the three major canyons of the Rio Grande in the Big Bend region, the Santa Elena was the most northerly. Looking toward the canyon's southerly end: "The very rock of Santa Elena seen from the desert downstream looked like a shimmering image of the heat. Sand, orange-colored foothills, blue haze in the canyon's mouth, all spoke of waste and heat, in immense proportions." (page 900) In May 1947 I could not draw the scale of the tawny rock; only try to imagine it from my sketch of its blanched colors, when writing my text later.

When a river's course is seen in its whole continuity, its physical character changes according to the variations of the lands through which it carves its way. The Rio Grande is born of mountains three miles high and on its long passage to the sea it flows by turns through canyons, deserts, and gardens. Below Del Rio, Texas, the river is a great silver vein bordered by the young green of groves in spring.

Rio Grande Below Del Rio
1950.
Watercolor, pastel,
13½ × 16¼" (sight).
Collection Mr. Dwight L. Hunter, Dallas

Referring to General Taylor's forces invading northern Mexico in summer, 1846: "The country they passed over was dead level, with unending clumps of mesquite. Those who kept up their journals every night had to write by the light of the new moon— there was too much wind to let them light a candle. So under a wide movement of air over the great empty plain the combat forces of the Army of the Rio Grande slowly faded out of sight into Mexico." (page 716) For the sense of vast space receding into the unknown, I had recourse to this image of the north Mexican plain drawn in midday from a height overlooking the river some miles below Laredo.

Looking Over North Mexico from Near Laredo, Texas
19 April 1949, 6:30 P.M.
Watercolor,
8½ × 10½"

Through local legend, I heard that smugglers used this bosky Rio Grande crossing northwest of Laredo, Texas. A *jacal*, or hut, on the Mexican side was a convenience in the flourishing and undisturbed trade.

Looking at Piedras Negras, Coahuila, from Eagle Pass, Texas, the Mexican town in its colored plasters in hot morning light. In 1867 the Emperor Maximilian was taken prisoner by the Mexican forces of Benito Juárez, and when the news of this "reached the river, a ball was given at the Customs House in Piedras Negras to which 'all the foreigners in Eagle Pass were invited . . . together with all the best people in that part of the country.'" (page 843)

Rio Grande at Eagle Pass/
Piedras Negras
23 April 1949, 9 A.M.
Watercolor, India ink,
Chinese white,
8½ × 10½".
Collection Mrs. Charles A.
Henderson, New York

Jacal *Across Rio Grande, Northwest of Laredo, Texas*
17 May 1949, 2 P.M.
India ink, colored pencil,
8¼ × 7⅞"

Río Grande at Eagle Pass - Piedras Negras 23 April 1949 R G. m.

The style of Spain—reflecting Moorish design—spoke in the doorway of the eighteenth-century church at Mission San Francisco de la Espada at San Antonio, Texas. Even in the Hispanic southwest, the cultural ancestry of Iberia was visible.

Among the "temples of San Antonio in their misty meadows" I saw "San Juan Capistrano with its uprolling facade pierced by arches." (page 336) The exuberant stone of the tower was an analogy for its architectural purpose—the lofting of bells and their song.

Bell Tower, San Juan Capistrano, San Antonio, Texas
8 April 1949, 4 P.M.
India ink, watercolor, Chinese white,
8½ × 10½"

Door of Mission San Francisco de la Espada, San Antonio, Texas
29 March 1949, 2:30 P.M.
India ink, watercolor, colored pencil, Chinese white,
9⅛ × 8½"

"San José, with its dome and carved tower and embrasures, and huge barrel-vaulted granary" (page 336) was built as the grandest mission community of the five established by the Franciscans at San Antonio in the eighteenth century. Here the Spanish colonial baroque found its richest expression, as I saw on a spring morning when the first green was coming on the mesquite.

Mission San José, San Antonio, Texas
29 March 1949, 9:20 A.M.
India ink, watercolor, Chinese white,
8½ × 10½"

Mier, the largest lower Rio Grande Mexican town after Matamoros, lay seven miles south of the river. A private chapel of the Valle family used the river sandstone "that weathered to a rich brown" (page 594), and though abandoned, its doors boarded up, it retained the grace of the colonial baroque and spoke of the remote society at its most ambitious.

Abandoned Private Chapel, Mier, Tamaulipas, Mexico
19 April 1949, 2:55 P.M.
India ink, watercolor, Chinese white,
8½ × 10½"

*"Oh, say, were you ever in Rio
    Grande?
Way, you Rio.
Oh, were you ever on that
    strand?
For we're bound for the Rio
    Grande.*
The chanty 'was heard on
the supply ships standing in
for General Taylor's depot
at Point Isabel.'" (page
661) In the war with
Mexico (1848–1849) the
United States forces found
their beachhead not at the
river's mouth but fourteen
miles east on the Gulf
Coast, where an old
masonry lighthouse, long
abandoned, evoked like a
witness in 1949 the history
that so fatefully had come
and gone.

Old Lighthouse, Port Isabel, Texas
16 April 1949, 4 P.M.
India ink, watercolor, Chinese white,
8½ × 10½"

Drifting on every road that meandered among the many channels of the river's estuary, I came along one that brought me into this meadow in which, apparently, sat an ocean-going freighter.

The Freighter California at Port Brownsville
14 May 6:00 pm 1947

Brownsville, Texas Port—Docked Freighter
14 May 1947, 6 P.M.
India ink, colored pencil,
8¼ × 7⅞"

Drawings for

CONQUISTADORS

IN

NORTH AMERICAN

HISTORY

Santa Fe, the Capital

of the Spanish Colonial kingdom of New Mexico, was founded in 1610. My thoughts often turned, in a sort of reverse journey, to the original Spanish invasion of Mexico in 1519, and to its northward consequences which culminated, a century later, in the precarious planting of the northernmost Spanish colonial capital—Santa Fe in the embrace of mountains named for the Blood of Christ. An arc of historical tension united La Rica Villa de la Vera Cruz on the Atlantic coast of Mexico to La Villa Real de la Santa Fe de San Francisco de Assisi in northern New Mexico.

Hernando Cortés landing at Vera Cruz with his little band of venturers on Good Friday in 1519 took the first step of the march of the conquistadors across Mexico and eventually through the generations toward North America. It was a journey I wanted to repeat in a book. Before I could do so, I must see the lands and feel the natural atmospheres of its enactment. As my stated purpose was to trace the conquest from New Spain to the north, I must begin, like Cortés, at Vera Cruz. From there his road—and mine—rose through dense jungle to bare volcanic flanks and heights, finally to wind across a great mountain spine and down into the Valley of Mexico. There I left him and followed his successors northward over a grand rolling sequence of desert plain, river valley, and mountain barrier—an earth design repeated again and again all the way into New Mexico. The arc of history took me over the road from Vera Cruz to Santa Fe. My drawings helped recall objects and airs of a journey which for me was four and a half centuries long.

Charles V, the Holy Roman Emperor, was also Charles I, King of Spain. Cortés must obtain from him the legal power to rule the conquest. It was long in coming, but "At last, in December 1522, a ship of Spain brought letters from Charles V. One officially appointed him governor and chief justice of New Spain. The other thanked him for his great services to the crown. He had come into his own. But royal caution was at work also, for the King sent to New Spain various officers of his own to administer certain departments of the colonial government . . . as though to limit the power granted to the Captain General, and to remind him where power came from." (pages 118–19) I tried to increase my understanding of this monarch by translating his portrait by Titian, whose paintings he loved.

Emperor Charles V
Drawn after a reproduction of the portrait by Titian. 1949.
India ink, watercolor,
10 ½ × 9 ½"

"The fleet came to harbor ▶ on Good Friday, 1519, the day of the True Cross, whereby they named their new port Vera Cruz. The protective island off shore they called San Juan de Ulúa." (page 32) Cortés later wrote to Charles V saying, "San Juan is not very safe and many ships were lost on account of the north winds which blow along that coast." Accordingly, the Spanish ships unloaded at Vera Cruz. San Juan, a fortress island, is now a Mexican naval station.

San Juan de Ulúa, Vera Cruz
22 May 1962, 12:30 P.M.
India ink, watercolor,
8 ¼ × 10 ⁹⁄₁₆"

S. Juan de Ulúa
V.C. 12:30 pm
22 April 62

Antigua Vera Cruz, an original stronghold of Cortés's forces, was abandoned as the greater coastal site of "the Rich City of the True Cross" flourished a dozen leagues to the south. On primitive inland roads I was guided to Antigua Vera Cruz and came upon a village of huts scattered in dense jungle about the Spanish baroque ruins. In dense twilight the stone façade with its devouring creepers and climbing roots opened on a forbidding darkness.

Antigua Vera Cruz—Spanish Masonry in the Jungle
21 May 1962, 5:30 P.M.
India ink, watercolor, colored pencil, Chinese white,
8¼×10½"

In the southern Mexico City suburb of Churubusco, the convent of San Matias and its chapel of San Antonio Abad were built by Franciscans in 1660. Fortified for defense in the War with Mexico in 1846, the premises were besieged and taken by General Winfield Scott's invading army. Now they are a historical museum. The chapel door was open and votive candles burned within as I painted.

Chapel of San Antonio Abad, Churubusco, Mexico City
1962.
India ink, watercolor, Chinese white,
13¾ × 10¾"

As I moved inland from Vera Cruz after Cortés, the Atlantic coastal plain began to give way to jungle slopes. In exhilarating freshness, the air carried the respiration of humid mountain greenings, and the fragrance of thousands of wild gardenias.

Fortín de las Flores, V.C., Mexico
22 May 1962, 7 A.M.
India ink, watercolor,
6×8"

In the Aztec village of Coyoacán the Conqueror established his headquarters. It faced the Emperor's city, which lay a few miles to the north. I drew a small excerpt of the municipal palace of the colonial government. The exuberant roofline and finials were characteristics of the art of the conquistadors.

Coyoacán—The Municipal Palace
1962.
India ink, watercolor,
6 × 8"

At one side of the vast central square of the Emperor's city of Tenochtitlán stood the greatest Aztec temple. Cortés pulled it down. The conquerors named the city Mexico. A Spanish church was built over the temple ruins with their stones. On the same site in 1573 a new cathedral was begun from designs drawn in Spain. It was completed two and a quarter centuries later. Arched vistas succeeded one another in my eye like recessions into the ages; and the grandeur of the silent organ and choir resonated for me with the voices of Mexico's pain and glory.

Portion of Organ and Choir, Cathedral, Mexico City
19 May 1962, 1:50 P.M.
India ink, watercolor,
10⅞ × 8½"

From a height overlooking ▶
the town of San Miguel de
Allende, dating from 1540,
I ventured on a general
view. Two principal
churches dominated the
lush valley—San Miguel,
with, it is said, the only
Gothic style in Mexico,
and Concepción, with its
tall dome.

***View of San Miguel de
Allende***
26 May 1962, 4:15 P.M.
Ballpoint pen, watercolor,
8 × 10"

26 May '12
4:15 pm

Paul

The Spanish genius for gardens created the Alameda as the long park of Mexico City. In 1839 Madame Calderón de la Barca "admired its noble trees, flowers, and fountains, all sparkling in the sun." (Fanny Calderón de la Barca, *Life in Mexico— Letters.* . . . New York, (1966.) Early on a May morning I walked across the park and came upon a church with a unique façade shaped like a concave shell. After drawing it for some while I was aware of being watched. Two very small boys stood behind me in rags. There was no one else to ask, so I asked them the name of the church. In unison they replied with miniature charm, "San Juan de Diós, Señor."

Ten years after Cortés came ashore at Vera Cruz, the site of Guanajuato was marked by northward explorers in 1529. A score of years later great veins of gold and silver were found there. I followed the winding streets of the old city. My drawing looked down through a narrow gateway and up over high walls to barren foothills beyond, and palisaded mountains. ▶

The Gateway, Guanajuato
27 May 1962.
India ink, watercolor,
6 × 8"

Church of San Juan de Diós, Mexico City
24 May 1962, 7:30 A.M.
India ink, watercolor,
11 3/8 × 9 3/8"

Santa fe
1880
memorial
Day.
Plaza.

White gloves.

U.S. Army soldiers, Santa Fe, 1880 (after Signal Corps photograph)

After the first period of northward exploration along the western marches of Mexico, the colonizing conquerors made their road up the central wastes of the great peninsula. Their outposts became fortified way stations, then towns, then cities. Riches of the earth created mining centers— Durango with its iron after 1563, Hidalgo del Parral, 1631, with its gold, silver, and baser metals. Such industries survive, as I saw in bright morning shadows.

Hidalgo del Parral, Chihuahua—the Mining Cut
30 May 1962, 7 A.M.
India ink, watercolor,
8¼ × 10½"

Reading back from this accoutrement of a horseman in the Spanish Colonial renaissance of North America, you can reconstruct something of his likeness and time. The stirrup bespeaks a character fond of a flourish, for there is a hole from which to lace a tassel. Soldier or householder, he was a man for an expedition. He was courageous and hardy, under his king, or he would not have been one who traversed oceans, deserts, mountains, rivers, to know his end across the world, leaving durable evidence of his passing this way—a chased metal stirrup north of the Rio Grande in Texas.

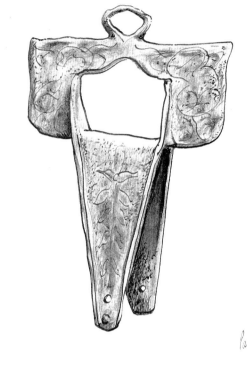

Spanish stirrup — one of a pair in Sul Ross Museum
16th Century
20 May 1947

Paul

Spanish Stirrup, 16th Century
20 May 1947.
Drawn after an object in the Museum, Sul Ross State University, Alpine, Texas.
India ink, colored pencil, Chinese white,
11 × 7⅞"

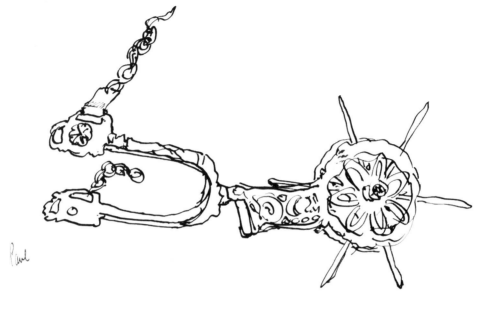

Spanish Spur found in the Chisos Mountains.
Sul Ross Museum.
24 April 1949

Spanish spur found in the Chisos Mountains, Rio Grande, Big Bend

The dust color of North Mexico lay over all I saw in Chihuahua. So it was then, and always was before, when the colonizers' trains moved along the trail to the Kingdom of New Mexico at the pace of its beasts of burden.

Chihuahua City, Mexico—Corona Mountain
30 May 1962, 12:30 P.M.
India ink, watercolor, Chinese white,
8¼ × 10½"

Overland travel in the colonial Kingdom of New Mexico followed many a grainy little valley like this one, where the hills above a struggling stream show as much gravel as grass, and the distance folds in upon itself time and again, just as the traveler believes the land is about to open out into long sight ahead—and a future.

New Mexico Valley
1965.
Watercolor,
7 3/8 × 9 7/8" (sight).
Collection Mr. and Mrs. Joseph W. Reed, Middletown, Connecticut

This is the sort of country that the colonizers saw on their final approach to the site of Santa Fe—red earth, scrub piñon trees, gullies for mountain runoff in summer rains, little valleys like fissures hidden in the wide openness of the plain of Santa Fe, which the Pueblo Indians who first knew the land called the Dancing Ground of the Sun.

View in La Cienega, New Mexico
1955.
Gouache on canvas,
5 × 6"
Collection Mr. and Mrs. Edward M.M. Warburg, Wilton, Connecticut

Mountains, mesas, other uplands seemed like eternal obstacles to the river in many places; but as such elevations rose in aeonial earth movements, the river, rather than coursing around them, cut through them, grinding its way with heavy sediment against layers of earth and rock to form canyons. The river came free of the canyon and flowed out into the desert plain. I drew a diagram of what the discoverers must have seen in their toiling marches. "An advance of five or six miles a day was gratifying; ten or twelve, very fast." (page 222)

Mesa Cut and River
1950.
India ink, watercolor,
9 × 12"

Drawings for

LAMY OF SANTA FE:

HIS LIFE AND TIMES

THE SUBJECT OF ARCHBISHOP LAMY of Santa Fe was part of my earliest experience in the old Spanish Colonial capital of New Mexico. Though he died in Santa Fe in 1888, the Archbishop left a living legacy to the city. Before 1920 I heard him spoken of there by people who had known him in their childhood and remembered him fondly.

Contrasting styles, French and Hispanic, were mingled with his legend after the benign young prelate arrived in 1851 to do the work of civilization as best he could with the materials at hand, in that land whose natural beauty surrounded a society provincial in all expressions and ways.

I felt through decades the need to trace his life in a biography. Finally, the task took me everywhere his life had taken him—his birthplace in Lempdes, near Clermont-Ferrand, in Auvergne; his passage through Paris on his way to America as a young missioner; his outland missions in central Ohio; his pastorate in Kentucky; his long first voyage to the Southwest by way of New Orleans and shipwreck in the Gulf of Mexico, then overland to El Paso and north to Santa Fe; his excursions in Colorado, California, Arizona, Mexico, Italy, and his native France. Further, he became a familiar traveler of the Santa Fe Trail. From all my observations and intuitions, beginning in my youth and occupying more than a quarter-century of my late years, grew my view of his life and lands.

Always in his background were the superb landscape of New Mexico, and the particular pungency of the old city of Santa Fe, where his nature, mortally joined to hers in 1888, remains a blessing.

"The family house sat flat-faced and flush with the other houses on its street. It presented a scatter of windows at random heights, some square, some small, others large and shuttered (oddly suggesting the fenestration in the church of Ronchamps by Le Corbusier of the twentieth century). A single-span door opened into the house at one end, and a wide double door at the other was the entrance to the concealed animal and wagon yard and barns behind. There were three low storeys, rising to the dusty vermilion roof like that over all the other houses."
(page 12)

Birthplace of Jean Baptiste Lamy, Lempdes, Puy-de-Dôme, France
23 June 1955, 4 P.M.
India ink, watercolor,
8½ × 10⅞"

"From childhood, Jean Baptiste Lamy, gazing from the tilled fields well to the north of Lempdes, across bluing hills, to the farthest line of the land where the solitary profile of the Puy-de-Dôme rose in the distance, could see between near and far the hazy cluster of the city of Clermont-Ferrand. The only constant and distinguishable features he could pick out were the two spires of the cathedral side by side, there, at the end of the country road leading from Lempdes to the city and the world. At that angle, in certain airs and lights, they might fancifully suggest the twin spires of a mitre, such as worn by a bishop, a lord and teacher." (page 23)

View of Clermont-Ferrand and its Cathedral From Fields North of Lempdes
23 June 1955.
Watercolor, pencil,
8 × 10¼"

The poignancy of leaving his homeland for unknown America touched Lamy deeply. I came upon a mid-nineteenth century photograph showing an ocean ship slowly making its way out of the harbor at Le Havre. It spoke to me of Lamy, aboard the *Sylvie de Grace* outbound, as "she made her way down bay, past the great stone fortress. . . . Presently the wind changed . . . and the wooden ship leaned and made for the open sea. . . . Not until night was falling did the voyagers lose sight of land as distance and darkness engulfed France." (page 22) I copied the photograph.

Sailing From Le Havre, 1839
n.d.
India ink wash on pink paper,
9½ × 10⅞".
Collection Mr. and Mrs. Joseph W. Reed, Middletown, Connecticut

On a pastoral tour of Arizona in 1853 Lamy came on the abandoned mission of Tumacacori which "gave evidence of a once beautifully designed and maintained outpost on the Santa Cruz River. But now its farm buildings, corrals, fences, bake-houses, and the large mission church with its little clay burial chapel within the cloister, were empty to the wind and sun and drifting desert. . . ." (page 312)

Tumacacori Mission, Arizona
6 March 1967.
India ink, watercolor, Chinese white,
9×12"

Guadalupe Range, New Mexico
23 March 1967, noon.
India ink, watercolor,
9 × 24"

"The caravaners . . . saw fifty miles to the north the Guadalupe Range with its highest point, Signal Peak, at its eastern end. It was on the crest of this peak that the Comanches built their signal fires on their autumnal strikes across the Rio Grande to steal Mexican horses, and it was that range which Indians used as sanctuary from which to raid passing caravans. The Guadalupes . . . were the first considerable mountains which Lamy saw on the boundary of his own domain. The military road—now abandoned—turned westward at the base of the Guadalupe foothills a hundred miles from El Paso del Norte." (page 103)

Working on my drawing, I saw no one, but I was seen. Out of nowhere a swarthy, smiling sexton appeared. He looked at my paper, nodded like an expert, and said, "But you work very fast," and with a frisk of his cassock went off to lock all the doors. When I realized what he was doing without giving me any warning—it was early evening and I was alone in the cathedral—I closed away my gear and made for the nearest open door.

Durango (City)—Cathedral Interior
28 May 1962, 7 P.M.
India ink, watercolor,
13¾ × 10¾"

Lamy was in the city of Durango in 1851 on a delicate and crucial mission: to secure from the Bishop of Durango the assignment of jurisdiction of the new vicariate apostolic of Santa Fe to himself, where formerly it had been held as part of the diocese of Durango whose bishop lived fifteen hundred miles away. The matter was amicably settled. Lamy looked about during his visit. The houses, "which if they were dirty outside were cleanly kept inside—though from a distance their white plaster showed handsomely under the hot sun. Lamy could see the great profile of the Sierra Madre to the west of town, across barren hills from which rose a curtain of dust." (page 145)

Durango (City)—Houses and Tower
29 May 1962, 9:30 A.M.
India ink, watercolor,
Chinese white,
8¼ × 10½"

Paul

Durango 24 May
9:30am '62

In 1854 Bishop Lamy was in Rome to fulfill his first *ad limina* visit to Pius IX. "The Pope signalized Lamy's audience in a superb and concrete fashion. He presented his forty-year-old bishop with a chalice out of the papal treasury. It was attributed to a goldsmith of the sixteenth century and spoke richly of Renaissance style in its design. Its height was over eleven inches. . . . It seemed clear that by a gift of such magnificence the Pope intended to show particular favor to his visitor, whose report of the desert diocese could refer to few enough of even the simplest sacred accessories." (page 204) I handled the chalice and made my drawing behind the altar in the Loretto Chapel, Santa Fe.

In 1858–59 Lamy's old schoolmate and ally, Father Joseph P. Machebeuf, with whom he had emigrated to America, was on a mission for the bishop which took him to Arizona and Mexico. He "moved on to Tucson, coming first to the decaying but spacious mission church of San Xavier del Bac, which had been built in the 18th century by Jesuits . . . He first saw it across parched yellow flats, as it stood white against bluing foothills and far purple mountains." (pages 263-64)

San Xavier del Bac, Tucson
9 March 1967, 1:30 P.M.
India ink, watercolor,
8 × 10"

Archbishop Lamy's Chalice
7 July 1968.
India ink, watercolor, colored pencil, Chinese white,
13⅞ × 11⅞"

78

San Francisco
Xavier del Bac
9 mai '67
1:30 pm

Diagram: fourteen arches, interior of Notre Dame de Port, Lempdes

In southwestern Kansas at a place now called the Ingalls Crossing of the Arkansas River, Lamy, leading a wagon train to Santa Fe in July 1867, met a party of hostile Indians. A seven-hour battle followed throughout a "terrible day." I told the story with my view of the battle site in mind. "The water ran, heavy with silt, in a channel which was part of a much wider dry bed. The approach where the wagons came was wide and sloping gradually to the ford. The opposite bank was more abrupt and the trail led from the river and past a grove of cottonwood trees. Tall fox-colored brush grew on both sides, and short, tawny grass, and prickly bushes with black stems and branches and parched leafage." (page 346)

Ingalls Crossing, Arkansas River, Kansas
29 March 1967.
India ink, watercolor,
9 × 12"

Northeast of Guaymas
about twelve miles from the
west coast of Mexico I saw
this storm of light in the sky
over a swayback mountain.

On the Way to Guaymas
3 March 1967.
Watercolor, pastel,
20⅛ × 26" (sight).
Collection Mr. Dwight L. Hunter, Dallas

In 1967 I was in pursuit of a church document vital to the legal definition of the southern portion of Lamy's New Mexico diocese. I heard that it could be found at Tucson. In Tucson I was directed to Alamos, in the state of Sonora, Mexico. My route there took me to Guaymas, on the Mexican coast, and thereafter inland to Alamos. At Alamos, the parish church (once a cathedral) had no records. I returned to Tucson and was greeted by a happy archivist who had found the document I needed. My pictorial note of Guaymas was an incident on the way.

View of Guaymas, Mexico, Across the Harbor
4 March 1967.
India ink, watercolor, Chinese white,
9 × 12"

"It was the poverty of the environment which prevented high aesthetic achievement of the Old World sort in the bishop's buildings. Falling between two traditions—the grand European and the uncultivated but fervent native—Lamy's style reached only a gesture and a function of devout memory. . . . Now, as the cathedral began to take shape, the Moorish arches of Spain, as repeated in the French Romanesque . . . began to show. [The bishop] estimated that the church would measure two hundred by sixty-six, 'all cut stone in the Roman Byzantine style.'"
(page 388)

Cathedral of St. Francis, Santa Fe, New Mexico—Exterior
1955.
India ink, watercolor,
3¾ × 5½".
Collection Mr. Charles D. Berke, Jr., Middletown, Connecticut

"Work was advancing on the nave in 1873, with a wide central aisle separated from two narrower side aisles by the first indications of plain stone columns, which were to be surmounted by semi-circular arches which recalled the interior of Notre Dame de Bonne Nouvelle at Lempdes. The adobe north transept and sanctuary of the old cathedral would have to remain part of the new." (page 389) My drawing looks across the sanctuary toward the north transept.

Cathedral of St. Francis, Santa Fe, New Mexico—Interior
9 July 1965, 10 A.M.
India ink, watercolor, gouache, charcoal,
14 × 10⅞".
Collection Mrs. Foster E. Zaiser, San Francisco

"The archbishop's throne was a walnut armchair carved in motifs of Victorian Gothic which rose along sides and top to a tall pinnacle flanked by finials resembling miniature pyramids connected by their bases. The arms, seat, and back were upholstered in dark cherry velvet bound by gold tape . . . surely the grandest piece of furniture in Santa Fe." (page 390) I found it in the sacristy of the cathedral.

Archbishop Lamy's Throne
6 January 1973.
India ink, watercolor,
13⁷⁄₈ × 10⁷⁄₈"

In 1869 Lamy was in Rome to attend the first Vatican Council. Always in search of scenes of his experience, I went to Rome in 1963 to see the Second Vatican Council in its second session to understand something of the atmosphere of such an event. My drawing looks toward the north transept of the basilica. "When the first Vatican Council was convened by Pius IX on 8 December 1869 in the wide and lofty north transept of St. Peter's, Lamy was in his place among the six hundred bishops in white mitres and copes who were seated on ranks of tribunes at right angles to the papal throne which stood at the far end of the chapel." (page 362)

St. Peter's Basilica, Rome—Interior
1963.
India ink, watercolor, charcoal,
11¼ × 8⅜" (sight).
Collection Mr. and Mrs. Samuel M. Green, Middletown, Connecticut

Mater Dolorosa (bulto), in the church at Tomè, New Mexico

A Vatican Council, assembling the Catholic bishops from around the world, is an august event. Lamy was present at the Council of 1869–70. When the Second Vatican Council was held in the 1960s, I felt that if I could gain admittance to it, I might feel something of what he experienced. Luckily I was declared *persona grata* and on Sunday, 29 October, 1963, I was present at the opening of the Council's second session, as Pope Paul VI, flanked by two cardinals, read his homily. Though I could see little more of him than his mitre and his eloquent left hand, I strongly had a sense of presence and occasion.

Pope Paul VI Opening the Second Session of the Second Vatican Council, St. Peter's, Rome
29 September 1963.
India ink, watercolor, Chinese white,
6 × 5½" (sight).
Collection Mr. and Mrs. Joseph W. Reed, Middletown, Connecticut

Lamy's travels were pro-
digious, and often plagued
by great hardships which,
in his frail constitution, he
faced down by sheer will. In
the southwest and Mexico
and over the plains he went
by horseback for tens of
thousands of miles. "Jerked
meat was common. He al-
ways carried some bread,
crackers, a few hard-boiled
eggs. It was all exhausting,
until in 1880 the railroads
came. He said, 'but look
back from the eighties to the
fifties, and it meant pur-
gatorial work.'" (page 419)
My drawing shows a stretch
of the railroad south from
Albuquerque to El Paso,
where in his late years
Lamy made rail connec-
tions for Mexico.

A.T.S.F.R.R. North of Socorro, New Mexico
15 October 1947, 11:30 A.M.
India ink, colored pencil

On the rising uplands of northern New Mexico the road aims at Lamy, the small railroad junction point for Santa Fe that was named after the bishop.

The Road to Lamy
19 May 1958.
Watercolor, pencil,
8¼ × 10¼".
Collection Mr. Charles D. Berke, Jr., Middletown, Connecticut

In 1959 I was in Paris before leaving for Rome to search for archives relating to Lamy. If in visiting Paris I always had a sense of returning to a place I had known long before, perhaps it was because as a boy I devoured the Valois novels of Alexandre Dumas, of which the historical center was the Louvre. A shadow of my early imaginative past is in this drawing.

Pavillon Marsan, Louvre
17 September 1963, 8 P.M.
India ink, watercolor, Chinese white,
7¼ × 10" (sight).
Collection Senator and Mrs. D. P. Moynihan, Washington, D.C.

In the autumn of 1959 I went from Paris to Rome by car. An important stop would be Lyon, where I was to see Cardinal Gerlier to ask for permission to consult archives that held references to Lamy. I detoured by way of the Loire and late one afternoon from the parapet of the Château of Amboise I wanted to keep the image of the castle, and the river beyond.

On the Parapet of the Château of Amboise
20 October 1959.
India ink, watercolor, Chinese white, colored pencil,
8 × 10¼" (sight).
Collection Senator and Mrs. D. P. Moynihan, Washington, D.C.

Returning from research travel in Europe I was about to sail from South-ampton in the *R.M.S. Queen Mary.* There was time enough to draw what I saw from the sun deck.

Tug and Tender, Southampton Docks
3 December 1959.
India ink, watercolor, Chinese white,
8 × 10¼" (sight).
Collection Senator and Mrs. D. P. Moynihan, Washington, D.C.

Acknowledgments

I MOST GRATEFULLY ACKNOWLEDGE the generous assistance of the following persons who at various stages and in a variety of ways fostered the development of this book: Charles D. Berke, Jr., Joaquin del Valle, Ralph Franklin, Paul Gottlieb, Clark Kimball, David McCullough, Ruth Peltason, and Christa Sammons.

My further thanks go to the following for permission to reproduce drawings from their collections: The Collection of American Literature, Beinecke Rare Book and Manuscript Library, Yale University; Charles D. Berke, Jr.; Mr. and Mrs. Samuel M. Green; Mrs. Charles A. Henderson; Dwight L. Hunter; Clark Kimball; Senator and Mrs. D. P. Moynihan; Mr. and Mrs. Joseph W. Reed; Mrs. Vitya Vronsky-Babin; Mr. and Mrs. Edward M. M. Warburg; Mrs. Foster E. Zaiser.